# COUNTERPOINT: ITALIAN
## © COUNTERPOINT NUTRITION LLC

*This book is dedicated to everyone who has--or will--
share a meal with us.
- Hollen and Joe*

# WHO WE ARE

We are two traveling, incorrigible, terminally curious and infectiously passionate chefs. With a combined twenty years of kitchen experience, we have amassed and honed a wealth of knowledge that is ever-growing and constantly being shared. Our journey of food and self-discovery has led us all over the world, working at incredible places, meeting inspirational people and eating as much as we can!

While on this journey we decided to get married—I asked, he finally caved—and as with most couples, looking good on our big day was important. Approaching traditional weight-loss protocol as chefs was at first disheartening: low-fat, no-fat, sugar-free, dairy-free, no booze, no fun...until we approached the process the same way we cook: creatively!

That's when we discovered ketogenic diets--omg cheese--just in time to do some research on our Italian honeymoon. Naturally our first book was inspired by our surroundings, and so began the conversation on of how to make Italian food ketogenic.

At first the idea sprang from the surprising way Italians eat. In America, Italian food tends to be starch, meat, bread, cheese, tomato sauce and wine, maybe basil on an adventurous day. In Italy the food changes from region to region; yes, there is pizza in Naples, but also seafood; Bologna gave us the most incredible lunch of an antipasti platter of sliced meats and spreads; Florentine steaks are to die for, and the quality of food at the grocery stores never failed to impress. This wasn't just a land of pizza, pasta and Olive Garden, it was a land of porchetta, aged vinegars, slow roasted vegetables, plates of pickles, whole fresh anchovies, and local, quality meats.

Italy was practically begging for a keto-adapted couple to scour it top to bottom, finding our favorite recipes and changing the perception of what ketogenic really is. Wanting to offer a counterpoint perspective of the ketogenic diet inspired us to write this book. We provide not only recipes, but also way to build whole meals, guides to building ketogenic antipasti boards, appetizers your guests won't know are on your diet, and entrees that are filling, healthy and still taste like Italy came over for dinner. There are even keto-friendly desserts!

We hope you enjoy the recipes inside this book as much as we enjoyed cooking them . Be sure to invite your family and friends to the table and wow them with the flavors from Italy we all love so much...from our table to yours.

## JOE & HOLLEN
## KOENIG

# TABLE OF CONTENTS

## WHAT IS KETOGENIC

The term ketogenic comes from the word "ketones", which are what truly feeds your body while you are in ketosis. When you burn fat, your body produces ketones, and these are what your cells use for energy. To be in Ketosis you need a high fat, low carb, and moderate protein diet. A keto diet is designed specifically to result in ketosis (to force your body to begin using fat for fuel instead of sugar, you have to restrict your carbohydrate intake and moderate how much protein you eat). Keep in mind that the amount of fat, protein, and carbohydrates vary widely from person to person and depending on metabolic needs. It can take anywhere from two weeks to two months to shift your body to burning fat as a primary fuel source and to experience all the benefits of being Keto-adapted. (We highly recommend reading the books "Keto-Clarity" or "The Art and Science of Low Carb Living" if you are interested in more information on Ketosis and living a Ketogenic life style.)

## WHY GLUTEN-FREE

After cooking the first few recipes in the Counterpoint Labs test kitchen we knew we were on to something delicious and healthy. We did not want to include any gluten in this book, as it is inherently against the idea of a low carb/ Ketogenic diet and much of the population does not do well with gluten via either sensitivity or allergy. The more research that is released, the more we realize the damage gluten is doing to our gut micro-biome as well as our overall health and wellness. Having been professional chefs for most of our lives we are no strangers to gluten-free guests, and wanted to give something tasty back to the community that has taken a lot of shit from chefs over the years.

# QUICK TIPS FOR USING THIS BOOK

**QUANTITIES**: The recipes in this book are built to feed four hungry adults (unless otherwise specified). If you are cooking for children or less voracious eaters than we, expect to have leftovers (you're welcome!)

**NUTRITIONAL FACTS**: All nutritional facts are based on average products. Mother Nature is not standardized, and variations will exist based on seasonality, breed of the animal/vegetable, brand of the product, and lots of other variations that exist in our food system. Do not take the nutritional facts as gospel.

**CARBOHYDRATES**: The debate rages over whether you should be counting total carbs or net carbs (total carbs minus fiber content). The nutrition facts in this book are *total* carbs. Your body reacts differently to different kinds of fiber, so we choose to use the true amount of carbs per dish; if you are on a strict ketogenic diet you should be keeping your total carbs under 50g per day. Once again this book is based on TOTAL CARBS, not net carbs.

**SALT**: Unless otherwise specified, we recommend using pink Himalayan salt. It is packed with minerals and electrolytes, it can help balance your hydration levels inside and outside of the cells, as well as boost your overall metabolism. You can use sea salt, kosher salt, or table salt in the recipes, adjusting your salt levels to your personal taste

**FAT VS. OIL**: Oils and fats all have different uses, flavors, and nutritional benefits that do not always play well with heat. In this book we wanted to make it easy: fats are for cooking and can be used in high heat applications while oils we classify for use in topping, marinades, and salad dressings. If the oil is not listed we recommend you try to avoid it.

FATS: Coconut oil, butter (grass-fed preferred), ghee, and bacon grease
OILS: Olive oil, macadamia nut oil, avocado oil, MCT oil, walnut oil, flax seed oil

**MEATS**: We recommend buying the best possible meat when you are able: pastured chicken, eggs, and pork, grass-fed beef, wild caught seafood (or open-pen, farm-raised fish), and wild game meats for flavor and healthy eating.

**VEGETABLES**: While organic is an easy way to ensure you are getting a cleaner and better product from the store, it is not always the best course of action. We recommend trying to find a farmers market or co-op near you that can provide you with better than organic: local, farm fresh vegetables, close to home.

**TOOLS AND TECHNIQUES**: If you don't know what something is "Google it"; if you don't understand a cooking technique, check it out on YouTube. We are in the information age and you have universal knowledge in your pocket; use it.

# ANTIPASTI

••••••••••••••••••••••••••••••••••••••••••••••••••••••••

*(in Italian cooking) an appetizer typically consisting of olives, vegetables, cheeses, and meats.*

*The greatest dishes are very simple.*

-Auguste Escoffier

# BUILDING YOUR OWN BOARD

## Antipasti Board

### CHEESE

Cheddar
Manchego
Parmesan
} *Hard*

Burrata
Chevre
Mozzarella
} *Fresh*

Brie
Camembert
Taleggio
} *Melty*

Bleu
Cotija
Feta
} *Crumbly*

Deli Cheese
Gouda
Provolone
} *Slicable*

### VEGGIES

Artichoke
Asparagus
Eggplant
Mushroom
Squash
Zucchini

### MEAT

Ham
Roast Beef
Turkey
} *Deli*

Building your own board is easy, fun, and a great way to start a meal. Use this handy guide to build your board by picking one or more items from each category and arranging them on a large wooden cutting board, platter, or stone. Use the recipes that follow to give your antipasti board a gourmet boost!

**SPREADS**

Savory Jam

Liver Pate

Roasted Garlic

Mustards

**NUTS**

Almonds

Macadamia

Pecan

Pistachio

Walnut

**PICKLES**

Capers

Cornichons

Pepperoncini

Pickled Veggies

Chorizo

Finocchio

Sopressata

Pepperoni

*Cured Sausage*

Bacon

Bresaola

Como

Prosciutto

Serrano

*Whole Cuts*

**OLIVES**

Castelvetrano

Kalamata

Marinated Mixed Olives

Stuffed Olives

# PREPARING SIMPLE VEGETABLES

Preparing good vegetables that even your kids will eat is not hard, as long as your main focus is preserving the integrity of the product. In laymen's terms: don't cook the crap out of your veggies!  They are beautiful, full of nutrients, and good for your body... what did they ever do to deserve being reduced to mush?!

This is a quick, straight-forward guide to grilling/roasting/sauteeing vegetables without vaporizing the flavor or texture. Today, we honor you humble vegetable; thanks for being awesome.

# FOR MOST VEGETABLES THERE ARE TWO SIMPLE WAYS TO PREPARE THEM:

1. WHOLE. Just put those suckers in a pan or on the grill with a little fat and salt and let them work their magic. As with all the techniques, the goal is to get grill marks on the veggies without burning them to death.

2. SLICED. These are the bigger vegetables that are too cumbersome to cook without paring them down to size. With larger veggies like eggplant, we usually slice them into rounds, but smaller squash and similar veggies can be planked to increase your grilling surface area. How you slice them is up to you, but after that, brush them with fat and salt, then quickly grill them for marks.

## WHOLE VEGGIES

Whether prepared on the grill, roasted quickly in the oven or sauteed on the stovetop, these guys are delicious with very little prep.

Asparagus

Green Beans

Green Onions

Mushrooms

Okra

Shallots

Spring Onion

Sunburst Squash

Tomatillo

## SLICEABLE VEGGIES

These vegetables we recommend slicing (S), quartering (Q), halving long-wise (H) or planking (P). Slicing usually refers to cutting across the vegetable, whereas planking refers to slicing the vegetable from top to bottom, long-wise.

Artickokes (H/Q)

Bok Choy (H)

Broccoli (P)

Cabbage (Q)

Eggplant (S)

Squash (S)

Zucchini (S/P)

# CHICKEN LIVER PATE

*These little pate jars are great as an evening snack with parmesan crisps, as a beautiful edition to an antipasti board, or an impressive holiday snack for guests. We like integrating liver into our diet because liver contains high-quality proteins, easily absorbable iron, and all the essential B vitamins including B12 and folic acid. They also have essential fatty acids, trace vitamins and minerals; yes liver can be delicious, give it a try!*

## INGREDIENTS

10 whole peppercorns

2 allspice berries

1 clove

5 coriander seeds

1/2 cup butter

1 onion, chopped

2 tsp salt

1lb chicken livers

1 T. Marsala

1/3 C. heavy cream

1 T fresh thyme leaves

## DIRECTIONS

1.    In a spice grinder, bullet blender or clean coffee grinder grind peppercorns, allspice, clove and coriander seeds. Pre-ground spices can be substituted, but season aggressively if this is the case.
2.    Sauté the onions in half of the butter and salt until soft and translucent.
3.    Add the livers to the pan and cook on med-high heat until the outsides are browned and the insides are still pink, 2-3 minutes per side.
4.    Remove from heat and add the splash of marsala. Madeira or dry sherry can be substituted.
5.    Blend mixture in a food processer on its lowest setting with remaining butter, heavy cream and fresh thyme. Season to taste with salt and fresh ground pepper and ensure it is smooth.
6.    Portion and smooth your delicious paste into a pretty container-- we like 4oz mason jars--and chill for at least 4-6 hours.

## SERVES 8

Calories: 219
Carbs:     1g
Protein:   9g
Fat:      21g

**Special Equipment**
**Spice Grinder + Food Processor**

Active Time: 10 minutes

Total Time: 6 Hours

# KETO CROSTINIS

*Living a low carb lifestyle can give you a unique perspective on the mechanics of eating certain foods like pate, really creamy cheese, and other dip style foods that can throw you for a loop; without crackers and bread as an intermediary how do you get these delicious foods from the bowl to your mouth without looking like a deranged cave man? These parmesan crisps will do the trick for most circumstances, plus you get to put cheese on your cheese!*

### YIELD: 2 DOZEN

## INGREDIENTS

2 C. Shredded parmesan cheese

Fresh ground black pepper

## DIRECTIONS

1.  Preheat oven to 400 degrees
2.  Use a tablespoon measuring spoon to portion out little piles on the silicone baking-mat lined sheet pan, at least 2" apart.
3.  Bake 6-8 minutes until golden brown and delicious.
4.  Let cool at least 5 minutes on the counter, then carefully remove from the pan.

Calories:   64
Carbs:      2g
Protein:    4g
Fat:        4g

**Special Equipment:**
**Silicon Baking Mat**

Active Time: 10 minutes

Total Time: 1 hour

# ROASTED GARLIC

*Who doesn't love a big soft clove of roasted garlic? It's like the bone marrow of the vegetable world: a spreadable bomb of pungent natural flavors. Roasted garlic is found on the olive bar in every fancy food grocery store, and while you certainly can spring for the no-muss, no-fuss approach, we prefer to roast it ourselves. It's cheaper, easy, and deceptively gourmet. It goes wonderfully on the antipasti board or spread by the clove on your steak--with garlic, you can't go wrong. If you want to make garlic oil, add an extra tablespoon of oil to the recipe.*

## YIELD: WHOLE GARLIC BULB

## DIRECTIONS

1. Preheat the oven to 350 degrees with a sheet pan inside.
2. Cut off the top of the garlic bulb so most of the individual sections are exposed. The goal is to barely expose the pockets of papery skin encasing the cloves so the oil can sink inside and they still steam inside the peel.
3. Pour olive oil onto a square of aluminum foil, season well with the salt and pepper and place the bulb upside down in the oil so the exposed cloves are sitting in the oil. Fold the aluminum foil so the garlic is sealed in tight and place the package in the oven so the bulb is right-side up again on the sheet pan, this lets gravity do the work of seasoning your garlic bulb for you.
4. Set timer for 35 minutes (don't forget to check for doneness and don't be afraid to roast longer).
5. When the garlic is done, remove it from the oven and let it cool before unwrapping—the steam is hot! Once roasted, garlic can be displayed as a whole bulb on an antipasti tray, or the individual cloves can be popped out of their sections and saved or enjoyed.

## INGREDIENTS

1 whole bulb of garlic

1 T. olive oil

Pinch salt

Pinch black pepper

## PRO-TIP:

If making infused oil, place cloves and roasting oil in a container and fill with fresh olive oil. We also like getting adventurous with our oils! Try tossing in a sprig of fresh rosemary, a lemon peel, whole peppercorns or whatever else is on hand.

Active Time: 10 minutes

**Special Equipment:**
None

Total Time: 1 Hour

| | |
|---|---|
| Calories: | 41 |
| Carbs: | 0g |
| Protein: | 0g |
| Fat: | 5g |

# KETO GARLIC BREAD

*Bread is always such a challenge when you're keto. Wikipedia says "bread was central to the formation of human societies"...holy cow! Giving up bread isn't just personally hard; it can feel like betraying your whole species. Maybe a bit dramatic but resisting garlic bread is hard, so we didn't! Here's our recipe for keto-friendly garlic bread.*

4/5, similar to frittata

## INGREDIENT

1 large head of cauliflower or 4 cups cauliflower rice

4 eggs

1 T good fat

2 cups mozzarella cheese

2 T. grated parmesan cheese

3 tsp dried Italian seasoning

4 cloves garlic, minced

1 tsp sea salt

1 tsp fresh black pepper

1 cup Colby Jack cheese

## DIRECTIONS

1.   Preheat oven to 425 F degrees with a cast-iron skillet inside.
2.   Ricing cauliflower: chop cauliflower into florets. Add the florets to your food processor and pulse until cauliflower resembles rice. How easy was that!
3.   Place the cauliflower in a microwavable container and cover with lid or plastic wrap. Microwave for 10 minutes.
4.   Once the cauliflower cools, dump it on a clean kitchen towel and squeeze out as much excess liquid as you can, don't use a paper towel it will rip and cauliflower will go EVERYWHERE.
5.   Place the cauliflower rice in a large bowl and add the eggs, mozzarella, Italian seasoning, garlic, salt and pepper. Mix everything together.
6.   Remove cast-iron from the oven and add the fat to it, giving it a minute to melt.
7.   Pour cauliflower mixture into the hot pan and spread evenly before replacing it uncovered back in the oven.
8.   Bake 25 minutes until golden brown and delicious
9.   Sprinkle with Colby jack cheese and put in the oven once more for 5 minutes until cheese has melted
10.   Slice and serve.

### SERVES 4

| | |
|---|---|
| Calories: | 236 |
| Carbs: | 4g |
| Protein: | 17g |
| Fat: | 17g |

**Special Equipment:**
**Cast Irong Skillet Or**
**Oven Safe Saute Pan**

Active Time: 30 minutes

Total Time: 1 Hour

# ZUPPA

·············································································

*A liquid dish, typically made by boiling meat, fish, or vegetables, etc., in stock or water.*

*Soup is a lot like a family.*
*Each ingredient enhances the others; each batch has its own*
*characteristics; and it needs time to simmer to reach full flavor.*

-Marge Kennedy.

# DOPE AF BONE BROTH

*Grandma was right all along: you just need some strong broth! Bone broth has been all over the news and in health magazines for years being heralded as a "cure all" for all kinds of illnesses and ailments. We highly recommend making a big batch once a month and freezing it; the process is labor intensive, so doing a large amount all at once will save you a chunk of time. While some of us are willing to work hard to make a truly amazing broth, others will want to take the short cut. I have included an easy to do slow cooker recipe that anyone can make with minimal effort, but warning: once you try the pro-version you won't want to go back.*

## YIELD: 12–15 CUPS

## INGREDIENTS

3 ½ lbs of beef bones

2 stalks of celery, chopped

1 medium onion, chopped

7 cloves of garlic, minced

2 bay leaves

2 tsp sea salt

1/4 C. apple cider vinegar

1/2 tsp dried rosemary

1/2 tsp dried marjoram

1 tsp dried thyme leaves

## DIRECTIONS (SLOW COOKER VERSION)

1.    Add all ingredients to a 6 quart slow cooker/crock pot and cover with cold water. Turn on high heat for one hour and skim off any foam that rises to the top.
2.    Reduce heat to low and let simmer covered for 24 hours.
3.    Once the bone broth has finished cooking, strain out the liquid, season to taste and put into containers. Once cool, label and freeze most of the broth, but keep in the fridge what you will want for the week.
4.    Heat a cupful in the microwave or on the stove when you want to enjoy the soothing and healing broth.

Calories:    72
Carbs:    1g
Protein:    4g
Fat:    6g

**Special Equipment:**
**Slow Cooker/Crock Pot**

Active Time: 30 minutes

Total Time: 24 Hour

# PRO DOPE AF BONE BROTH

## YIELD: 32 CUPS

## DIRECTIONS

1. Preheat your oven to 375 degrees and coat the knuckle bones in the coconut oil. Lay the knuckle bones and marrow bones on a large pan and roast for one hour.
2. While the bones are roasting, toss the onions, celery, carrots, garlic, and tomato paste in a bowl and mix thoroughly.
3. Remove the bones from the oven (should be well browned) and add to a large stock pot with 11qts of cold water. Place on the stove at medium high heat; reserve the fat and drippings in the roasting pan.
4. Add the vegetables and tomato paste mixture to the roasting pan with the fat and drippings from the bones and scrape the bottom of the pan with a metal spatula or wooden spoon to help get the drippings mixed into the vegetables. Roast in the oven for 20-30 minutes until the color is dark brown.
5. While the vegetables are browning, your water should be coming to a simmer and foam should be rising. As it does, skim it off with a mesh strainer or fine slotted spoon and discard.
6. After an hour of simmering and skimming, add the vegetables from the roasting pan to the stock pot. Take the remaining 1qt of cold water and pour it into the roasted pan to deglaze; using the spatula or spoon, scrape the bottom to release all the flavor stuck to the bottom and add it to the stock pot (*pro-tip: use wine instead of water at this step!)
7. Add all remaining ingredients to the pot, turn the heat down to low and cover the pot.
8. Let sit on stove for 24 hours, stirring every 8 hours.
9. Once the bone broth has finished cooking, strain out the liquid, season to taste and store in containers to cool. Label and freeze most of the broth. Keep in the fridge what you will want for the week.
10. Heat up a cupful in the microwave or on the stove when you want to enjoy the soothing and healing broth.

## INGREDIENTS

10 lbs beef knuckle bones

5 lbs beef marrow bones

2 T. coconut oil

4 C. onions, chopped

2 C. celery, chopped

2 C. carrots, chopped

4 garlic cloves, crushed

1/2 C. of tomato paste

2 Bay leaves

1/2 tsp dried thyme

1/2 tsp dried rosemary

1/2 tsp black pepper corns

2 whole cloves

6-8 parsley stems

1/2 C. apple cider vinegar

1 T. sea salt

12 qts of cold water

Active Time: 2 Hours

Total Time: 26 Hours

**Special Equipment:**
**LARGE stock pot**

Calories: 85
Carbs: 1.5g
Protein: 4g
Fat: 6g

# CREAM YOURSELF KETO

*Since going keto, one of my favorite soups is back on the menu: Cream Of. Nope, not missing a word there, we love "cream of" soups: cream of mushroom, cream of broccoli, cream of celery, cream of asparagus...really can't go wrong. The only real restriction for this style of soup is the thickening agent, but there's an easy way around that, too! Most "cream of" soups call for a roux to thicken them, or even corn starch, but the best way to get the most out of your soup is to use the vegetables themselves as filler. This means watching the amount of broth or stock to make sure it doesn't thin the pureed mixture too far, and blending the veggies extra smooth.*

## INGREDIENTS

3 T. butter

1 onion, chopped

3 ribs of celery, chopped

1 tsp salt

2-3 C. main attraction vegetable

1-3 C. stock or broth

1/2-1 C. heavy cream

salt and pepper to taste

### SERVES 4

## DIRECTIONS

1.    Sweat (saute until soft) the onion and celery in the butter with the salt.

2.    Add the main attraction veggie and sweat. If using something like onion, mushroom, celery, zucchini or any other vegetable with significant water content, then sweat until juices are released.

3.    Add stock just to cover vegetables and simmer until tender--be careful not to overcook!

4.    Blend soup in batches or with an immersion blender.

5.    If serving immediately, add heavy cream, gently heat and season with salt and pepper to taste.

**Nutrition facts vary**

**Special Equipment:**
**Blender/Immersion Stick**

Active Time: 10 minutes

Total Time: 1 Hour

## SOUP AND GARNISH OPTIONS:

- Cream of asparagus: drizzled olive oil and cracked fresh pepper

- Cream of broccoli: fried tiny florets of broccoli

- Cream of cauliflower: a pinch of smoked paprika

- Cream of celery: save the tender yellow inner celery leaves

- Cream of eggplant: lemon zest and a pinch of cayenne

- Cream of fennel: use bulbs for the soup but save feathery fronds to garnish

- Cream of mushroom: sauté fresh mushrooms with truffle oil and parsley

- Cream of spinach: ground nutmeg

- Cream of zucchini: ground nutmeg and pinch of cayenne

## PRO-TIP 1:
If making soup to save for later, add cold heavy cream to keep the soup from overcooking.

## PRO-TIP 2:
With green soups like cream of asparagus, celery or zucchini, add a handful of spinach when blending to brighten up the green without losing too much flavor while adding great phytonutrients.

# LOW-CARB WEDDING SOUP

*We love Italian wedding soup because of its simplicity and the fact that's it's a customizable dish. The term "Italian wedding soup" has to do with the marrying of meat and vegetables in broth, not someone's actually nuptials. Most restaurants in the United States add some kind of pasta or beans to the soup, while those living a low-carb lifestyle usually just omit the two; we thought it would be fun to add a little more substance to the soup to make a hearty meal with the addition of mushrooms and zucchini noodles.*

## INGREDIENTS

1/2 lb ground beef

1/2 lb ground pork or lamb

2 T. yellow onion, minced

3 garlic cloves, minced

2 T. flax seeds, ground

1 whole egg

1 tsp red pepper flakes

1/2 tsp ground black pepper

1 tsp sea salt

1 tsp fresh thyme leaves (1/2 tsp dry if you don't have fresh)

1 tsp fresh Oregano leaves (1/2tsp dry if you don't have fresh)

## PALEO GARLIC MEATBALLS

## DIRECTIONS

1.    Preheat oven to 365 degrees
2.    Mix all ingredients together into a bowl and thoroughly combine, form into small balls for the soup so one will comfortably fit onto a soup spoon.
3.    Place on an oiled baking sheet and bake for 25 minutes, let cool on the counter top while you make the following soup recipe.

# Everything Else

## Directions

1.  Render/liquefy fat in a heavy bottom soup pot or dutch oven at medium heat, add onions and celery, stir often while cooking for about 5 minutes (onions should be translucent).
2.  Add garlic and mushrooms to the pan and continue to cook for another 3 minutes or until the mushrooms are mostly cooked (go ahead and eat one to test it out).
3.  Add in the rosemary, oregano, black pepper, and red pepper flakes and cook for another minute or so, just enough to release the oil from the herbs and spices.
4.  Pour in your bone broth + water or strong broth to the pot, then add your meatballs, cover and let sit at medium low heat for 20 minutes to let the flavor marry... see what I did there.
5.  Add in all remaining ingredients and let cook on medium low for another 10 minutes to allow the kale to cook and the zucchini noodles to absorb the flavor of the broth
6.  Taste the broth and adjust the salt as needed, pour into bowls and garnish with parmesan cheese.
7.  Enjoy this tasty bowl of Ketogenic marital bliss

## Ingredients

1 T. fat

1 C. onions, chopped

½ C. celery, chopped

1 C. mushrooms, sliced

4 cloves of garlic, minced

1 T. Rosemary leaves, chopped

1 tsp oregano leaves, chopped

1 tsp black pepper

1tsp red pepper flakes

4 C. Bone broth + 2C Water

(or 6C strong beef broth/stock)

Paleo Garlic Meatballs
(previous page)

2 C. zucchini noodles cut 1"

in length

Leaves from the celery stalks

1 C. of chopped Kale

4 basil leaves, torn

Salt to taste

Parmesan cheese to garnish

(opt.)

### Serves 4

Active Time: 40 minutes

Total Time: 1 Hour 20 minutes

**Special Equipment:**
**Vegetable Spiralizer**

Calories:  156
Carbs:     4g
Protein:   20g
Fat:       6g

# MUSHROOM CHEESE FONDUTA

*This soup is great for cheese addicts, which we definitely are. Feel free to experiment with the cheese in your fonduta; we just use whatever little odds, ends and rinds are left over from a party or other recipes. This is a really impressive soup to start a meal, as a stand-alone or even a small soup shooter--put those old shot glasses from college to good use. The only "fancy" ingredient is the truffle oil, and don't skimp on that! One small bottle will last forever and it's an easy way to class up any dish. And remember that tip about saving roasted garlic cloves from a few pages back...? Add a clove to the fonduta for extra POW!*

## INGREDIENTS

2 T. butter

2 T. olive oil

10 oz. (3 C.) mushrooms, sliced

3 celery ribs, thinly sliced

1 leek, cleaned and thinly sliced

4 c bone broth

2 sprigs thyme

1 bay leaf

1 clove roasted garlic

1 3" piece of hard cheese rind

Salt and fresh ground pepper

1/2 c heavy cream

1/2 c grated cheese (Gouda, Mild White Cheddar, or Parmesan are great choices)

Chopped parsley and truffle oil to garnish

| Calories: | 329 |
|---|---|
| Carbs: | 2g |
| Protein: | 12g |
| Fat: | 25g |

## DIRECTIONS

1.  Heat butter and olive oil to sauté mushrooms until lightly browned--4-5 minutes stirring occasionally. Add the celery and leek, lower heat and sweat vegetables until tender but not browned, 5-7 minutes.
2.  Add chicken stock, thyme (saving a few leaves for garnish), bay leaf, garlic clove and cheese rind (we used Parmesan), simmer 30 minutes.
3.  Remove thyme, bay leaf and cheese rind and blend soup in batches or with stick blender until smooth, season to taste with salt and fresh ground pepper.
4.  Bring cream to a boil, remove from heat, stir in cheese until melted and smooth.
5.  Portion soup into bowl and drizzle fonduta generously into each serving. Garnish with light drizzle truffle oil and thyme leaves and serve immediately.

## SERVES 4

**Special Equipment:**
**Blender/Immersion Blender**

Active Time: 30 minutes

Total Time: 1 Hour

# Enjoying the book so Far?

*Be sure to check out all of our recipes, cooking tips, and biohacks at:*

www.counterpointnutrition.com

# COUNTERPOINT
# NUTRITION

# INSALATA

........................................................

*We don't need a melting pot in this country, folks. We need a salad bowl. In a salad bowl, you put in the different things. You want the vegetables--the lettuce, the cucumbers, the onions, the green peppers--to maintain their identity. You appreciate differences.*

-Jane Elliott

# KETO KALE CAESAR

*The Caesar dressing lends itself to Keto very nicely, and with a few tweaks you can have yourself a delicious and nutritious salad that is at home on its own for lunch with some grilled chicken thighs, bacon, or salmon, or as a side salad for dinner. We prefer to maximize the nutritional value of dishes and use healthier ingredients when we can, so this Caesar is made with kale to give you a dark green boost of vitamins, micronutrients, and polyphenols. Enjoy!*

## MCT CEASAR DRESSING

### INGREDIENTS

1 pastured egg yolk

2 tsp minced garlic

1 tsp Dijon mustard

Juice of 1 lemon

4 anchovy filets

1 dash Worcestershire sauce

1 tsp champagne vinegar

1/4 C. extra virgin olive oil

1/4 C. MCT oil

2 T. grated parmesan cheese

### DIRECTIONS

1.　In a small bowl combine: mustard, garlic, champagne vinegar, lemon juice, anchovies, egg yolks, black pepper & Worcestershire sauce. Blend with an immersion blender until smooth. Slowly add oils with the immersion blender on to form an emulsion, using small amounts of warm water to thin out if the mixture becomes solid and stops moving from the blender.

2.　Finish by stirring in the cheese by hand. Store in refrigerator until you need it; this will yield more than enough for a few salads and stays good in the fridge for 5 days.

## CHIA SEED CROUTONS

### INGREDIENTS

1/2 C. ground chia seeds

1/4 C. coconut flour

1 T fresh chopped rosemary

1 tsp thyme leaves, picked

1 tsp GF baking powder

1/2 tsp sea salt + 1/2 tsp sea salt

4 whole eggs

1 C. extra virgin olive oil

1 T. minced garlic

### DIRECTIONS

1.　Preheat the oven to 350 and line a sheet pan with parchment paper
2.　Combine chia seeds, rosemary, baking powder, and 1/2 tsp salt in a small bowl. Mix together until well incorporated.
3.　In a large bowl combine eggs and 1/2 C. of olive oil, whisk together then add the dry ingredients, stirring to mix together.
4.　Pour out the mixture onto the baking sheet and smooth even. It may not fill the pan, but your goal is to keep it 1/2" thick. Bake for 20 minutes.
5.　Let the dough cool on the counter until it reaches room temperature before cutting into cubes; place the cubes into a large bowl and turn the oven up to 400.
6.　In a separate bowl mix together the minced garlic, extra salt, olive oil, add the croutons and toss gently with your fingertips. Pour the croutons back onto the baking sheet and put in the oven for 5 minutes, open the oven and stir the croutons around, continue to cook for another 5 minutes.

# SALAD ASSEMBLY

## DIRECTIONS

1.     Mix the kale in a large bowl with 1/4 C. of the dressing and let sit for five minutes. This helps the kale to break down a little and provides a nicer texture.
2.     Add the chia seed croutons, the parmesan cheese and toss until well coated.

### SERVES 4

## INGREDIENTS

1 whole bulb of garlic

1 T. olive oil

Pinch salt

Pinch black pepper

## PRO-TIP 1:

If the croutons are intimidating feel free to substitute the parmesan crisps on p. 10. The combination of the fresh and the crisp parmesan is divine!

## PRO-TIP 2:

You can make the dressing and croutons separately and only mix in what you need in a lunch-for-one or dinner-for-two scenario. Save the components seperately to extend the shelf-life of your salad!

Active Time: 1 Hour (5 min. if croutons and dressing are made)

Total Time: 90 Minutes

**Special Equipment:**
**Blender/Immersion Blender**

Calories:   382
Carbs:       10g
Protein:     9g
Fat:           36g

# EASY CAPRESE

*This is an Italian staple and for good reason, it is simple and delicious just like all great dishes from the Old World. Garden fresh tomatoes with bright basil, creamy mozzarella cheese, some vinegar and good quality olive oil is all it takes to whip up one of our favorite lunch items. Traditionally you find balsamic vinegar on this dish, but balsamic has a few too many carbs for us, so we went with red wine vinegar instead.*

## INGREDIENTS

1 lb of fresh mozzarella cheese

1 large tomato from the list above (two if you are using plum tomatoes)

8 basil leaves

1/4 C. good quality olive oil

2 T. red wine vinegar

4 C. of your favorite lettuce

Pinch of salt

Fresh cracked black pepper

SERVES 4

*When it comes to choosing your tomato we recommend the following sliding scale based on total amount of carbs and flavor:

1.  Yellow Heirloom tomato
2.  Red Heirloom tomato (the lighter color = less sugar i.e., less carbs)
3.  Kumato tomatoes
4.  Italian Plum tomato
5.  To hell with it, any tomato will do if you got this far down the list!

## DIRECTIONS

1.  Slice the tomatoes in ½ inch rounds, then cut the round in half to create half moons (unless you used smaller tomatoes, then leave in rounds).
2.  Slice the mozzarella into ¼ inch rounds (should yield about 16 slices).
3.  Put the spring mix in the middle of a platter and alternate a tomato and piece of mozzarella until you cover the whole bottom of the spring mix.
4.  Drizzle the olive oil and vinegar over the whole platter (be sure to get some on top of the spring mix), sprinkle the salt and cracked black pepper over the tomatoes and mozzarella.
5.  Tear the basil leaves by hand into little pieces and sprinkle them all over the salad mix, mozzarella, tomato, and the negative space on the platter to make it beautiful. Place in the middle of the table with a serving spoon and let your guests marvel at your culinary badassery!

Calories: 275
Carbs: 5g
Protein: 12g
Fat: 24g

**Special Equipment:**
**None**

Active Time: 10 minutes

Total Time: 10 minutes

# How-To Garden Salad

*Salads are easy, fun to make for all ages, and a great way to utilize leftovers. This is a basic setup for a solid Italian garden salad that will look great on the table and be tasty in your mouth. Follow the recipe below to make a base salad and then add anything else you'd like from leftover vegetables, meats, cheeses, or anything your mind can think up.*

## Basic Salad Mix

### Ingredients

5 oz package of mixed greens

1/4 of a red onion, thinly sliced

12 cherry tomatoes, cut in half

1/2 of a cucumber, thinly sliced

6 pitted kalamata olives, cut in half

6 pitted green olives, cut in half

1/4 C. Italian-style dressing (recipes below)

### Classic Italian Dressing

3 T. coconut vinegar (or white wine vinegar)
1 tsp Dijon mustard
1/2 tsp onion powder
2 cloves of garlic, minced
1/2 tsp dried thyme leaves
1/2 tsp dried basil
1/2 tsp dried oregano
1/2 tsp sea salt
1/2 tsp black pepper
2 T. extra virgin olive oil
2 T. MCT oil

1. Add all ingredients except oil into a small bowl, whisk together, slowly add the oils while whisking to fully incorporate.

Active Time: 10 minutes

Total Time: 10 minutes

Below are three additional different styles of dressings you can make using MCT oils. "MCT" or medium-chain triglycerides are a form of saturated fatty acid that are present in 60% of coconut oil. MCTs are easily digested by your liver and turned directly into energy through the breakdown of fats in ketones. They are thermogenic which means it speeds up the metabolism and makes you burn fat more efficiently.

### Directions

1. Toss ingredients together in a large bowl, top with dressing of your choosing, serve. It's an easy salad, don't over think it.

| MCT Garlic Dressing | Creamy Basil Dressing |
|---|---|
| 8 cloves of roasted garlic (page 11) | 1/2 avocado |
| 3 T. red wine vinegar | 2 T. apple cider vinegar |
| 1 T. Dijon mustard | 1/4 C. extra virgin olive oil |
| pinch of Stevia or Xylitol | 2 T MCT Oil |
| 1 T. fresh lemon juice | 6-8 basil leaves |
| 3 T. extra virgin olive oil | |
| 3 T. MCT Oil | |

1. Combine all ingredients except for the oil in a blender (or a bowl with an immersion blender), blend until smooth, slowly adding in oil with your blender on its lowest setting. Store in a mason jar or airtight Tupperware until use.

### Serves 4

**Special Equipment:**
**None**

| | |
|---|---|
| Calories: | 162 |
| Carbs: | 5g |
| Protein: | 0g |
| Fat: | 14g |

# PRIMI

....................................................

*A small savoury dish forming the **first** of the successive parts of a meal.*

*Food for the body is not enough. There must be food for the soul.*

-Dorothy Day

# Spaghetti Squash Bolognese

*Time to banish the gluten and carbs in pasta and turn to the often overlooked and beautiful spaghetti squash. These big yellow gourds are delicious and shred into spaghetti all on their own with just the stroke of a fork. The noodles themselves work great for all kinds of pasta dishes, but we think they taste best with our Bolognese sauce!*

**SERVES 4**

## Preparing the "spaghetti"

### INGREDIENTS

2 tsp sea salt

1/2 tsp black pepper

2 T. fat

1 tsp crushed garlic

### DIRECTIONS

1.  Preheat the oven to 350 and cut the squash in half, removing the seeds with a spoon.
2.  Mix 1 T. fat, 1 tsp salt, and 1/2 tsp of black pepper; pour over squash halves.
3.  Place in the oven to bake for 1 hour; remove and let cool.
4.  Scrape the flesh of the squash into a large bowl.
5.  Just before serving, take the other 1 T. oil, 1tsp salt and garlic and place into a large sauté pan on medium high heat. Once the garlic begins to smell add your spaghetti squash and toss a few times to get it hot (about 3 minutes)
6.  Portion out the noodles onto four plates and top with the A-OK Bolognese.

# A-OK BOLOGNESE

## DIRECTIONS

1.    Heat a Dutch oven or a large heavy bottom pot to medium high, add the ground beef and cook until about ¾ of the way cooked (mostly brown a little pink is ok). Lower the heat to medium.
2.    Add the onions and celery to the pot and continue to cook for about 5 minutes.
3.    Pour in the vinegar, tomatoes, olive oil, herbs, salt, and pepper.
4.    Continue to cook on medium for another 10 minutes (this is a great opportunity to finish up the spaghetti squash noodles). Taste to check that you have the right amount of salt and pepper and serve over the spaghetti squash noodles.

## INGREDIENTS

1 lb ground beef

1 tsp sea salt

1/2 tsp fine ground black pepper

1/2 C. yellow onion, diced

1/4 C. celery, diced

2 T. garlic, minced

2 T. red wine vinegar

1 T. olive oil

1 C. crushed tomatoes

1 tsp thyme leaves

1 tsp oregano (dried or chopped fresh)

1T. basil leaves, chopped

## PRO-TIP:

Date night? In-laws coming over? Or maybe you just want to class it up and treat yourself! Either way, make that dish look fancy by spooning plenty of bolognese over the warmed squash and top with fresh shaved parmesan (use a vegetable peeler for an extra-refined look) and torn or sliced basil leaves. Bonus points for fresh cracked pepper and an olive oil drizzle!

Active Time: 30 minutes

Total Time: 90 minutes

**Special Equipment:**
**None**

| | |
|---|---|
| Calories: | 332 |
| Carbs: | 12g |
| Protein: | 23g |
| Fat: | 22g |

# VEGETABLE LASAGNA

*Lasagnas are not quick, they take some time, love, and assembly to properly pull off. Our vegetable lasagna uses multiple techniques and vegetables to bring a complex and delicious flavor to the dish. This lasagna is low carb and Keto-friendly, it uses broth to cut down on the sugar and carbs from the tomato sauce, and with noodles made out of vegetables, you can rest easy knowing you and your table mates are getting tons of vitamins and prebiotic fiber! Feel free to add some ground beef or bacon to your sauce if you are a ravenous carnivore, but we love this dish with all its vegetable glory!*

## FENNEL SALT

2 T. Fennel seeds

1/2 C. Kosher Salt

**SERVES 4**

1. Toast fennel seeds quickly in a pan, about two minutes.
2. Combine with kosher salt.

## VEGETABLE PREP

1 medium eggplant

1 medium zucchini

1 medium yellow squash

1 C. sliced mushrooms (we like criminis)

1/2 C. olive oil

1 T. fennel salt

1/2 tsp cracked black pepper

## DIRECTIONS

1. Preheat the oven to 375. Cut the ends off eggplant, then slice lengthwise into 1/4-inch-thick slices (discarding peel-covered ends). Lay slices on a rimmed baking sheet and sprinkle both sides liberally with salt; this helps to release the natural bitterness of the eggplant. Let stand for 15 minutes and then rinse salt off under cold running water and pat slices dry.
2. While the eggplant is draining, slice the zucchini and squash into ¼" thick planks.
3. In a small bowl mix together salt, pepper, and olive oil, brush the oil on to each side of the vegetable planks and lay on an aluminum foil-lined baking sheet (don't crowd the pan; use two pans if you need to).
4. In the bowl of the left over oil, toss in the mushroom and put on one of the pans. Put all vegetables in the oven and roast for 15 minutes. Remove from oven and let cool on counter for 20 minutes

## RED SAUCE

2 T. fat

1/2 C. yellow onion, diced

2 T. garlic, minced

1/2 C. canned tomatoes, crushed

1/2 C. bone broth

1 T. tomato paste

Salt and pepper to taste

## DIRECTIONS

1. Put your fat in a small sauce pan on medium high heat, Once the fat has come to temperature add your onion and cook for 3 minutes. Add in the garlic and cook until the garlic browns just the slightest bit, about 2 minutes.
2. Add in the broth and tomato paste, whisk together and cook until the broth is reduced by half.
3. Reduce heat to low, add the tomatoes and Italian seasoning. Let cook on low for 5 minutes and then turn off heat and let sit until ready to assemble.

## RICOTTA MIXTURE

2 C. ricotta cheese

## EXTRA ASSEMBLY ITEMS

1 pastured egg

2.5 C. mozzarella Cheese

2 T. parmesan

2 C. spinach leaves

1/2 tsp fennel salt

2 T. grated parmesan cheese

1/4 tsp fresh ground nutmeg

1.    Mix all ingredients in a small bowl, whisk together until well incorporated, set in refrigerator until ready to assemble.

## FINAL ASSEMBLY

1.    Preheat the oven to 350.

2.    Grease a loaf pan and put the eggplant slices at the bottom of the pan,  top with 1/2 C. of the ricotta mixture, top that with 1/2 C. of fresh spinach leaves, top the spinach with 1/2 C. of mozzarella cheese, then top that with 1/4 C. of red sauce.

3.    Repeat the process with the yellow squash, then the zucchini, and then the mushrooms, topping each layer of vegetables with the instructions from above.

4.    Once you reach the top add an additional ½ C. of mozzarella cheese to the top and finish with the grated parmesan.

5.    Cover and bake in the oven for 45 minutes; uncover and bake an additional 10 minutes. Let cool for twenty minutes, slice, and serve.

## PRO-TIP:

If you have leftovers of this lasagna, cut cold and put on a plate, top with a ¼ cup of mozzarella cheese and microwave for 3 minutes, it's a bubbly delicious leftover dish that works great in a Tupperware for work.

Active Time: 60 minutes

Total Time: 2 hours

**Special Equipment:**
**Loaf Pan**

Calories:    497
Carbs:    11g
Protein:    21g
Fat:    39g

# KETO CARBONARA

*Many people find it hard to get enough fats in their diet when first starting a full ketogenic diet, but this dish will do the trick every time! Carbonara in Italy does not come with cream; it was is assumed to be an American addition to this classic dish that traditionally relies on the bacon fat and egg yolks to coat the noodles rather than the cream, but hey--cream is delicious and it is full of keto friendly fat!*

## INGREDIENTS

### Zoodles

One medium zucchini per person, medium cut on a spiralizer

1/2 tsp sea salt

### Carbonara Sauce

4 slices bacon, diced

1 C. heavy cream

2 egg yolks

+1 yolk per person for garnish

2 tsp minced garlic

1 tsp cracked black pepper

1/2 C. grated parmesan cheese

### SERVES 4-6

## PRO-TIP:

I find the easiest way to separate the egg without breaking the yolk is to simply use your hands!

## DIRECTIONS

1.    Sprinkle the salt onto the zoodles and mix thoroughly in a bowl, let sit for 15 minutes. Then pour out all the liquid, ensuring a salted and dryer zoodle.

2.    Mix the two egg yolks with the heavy cream in a bowl and whisk vigorously, keep to the side.

3.    While the zoodles are draining, add your bacon to a non-stick pan on medium heat, let render and cook to just done and not too crispy as we will cook this again (about 8-10 minutes). Remove the bacon and fat keeping the two separate, add ½ of the bacon fat back to your pan keeping the heat at medium.

4.    Add your zoodles to the hot bacon fat in the pan and sautée for 3 minutes, just enough for the zucchini to cook slightly and to absorb some of the bacon fat. Strain the zoodles out and discard the liquid.

5.    Wipe your non-stick pan out with a towel and put back on the stove at medium-high heat. Add the other ½ of the bacon fat to the pan along with the cooked bacon and garlic, sauté for 3 minutes or until the garlic starts to change color, add your heavy cream and egg yolk mixture--stirring constantly--and let cook for 2 minutes.

6.    Add the parmesan cheese to the sauce and let reduce for another 3 minutes, stirring the whole time. Add in the fresh cracked black pepper and zoodles, sauté until the noodles are covered and the sauce is not runny. Plate like a nest in the center of the plate.

7.    Separate one egg yolk at a time, discarding the white, and very carefully run a little hot water over the yolk to remove any of the white stuck onto it. Add the yolk to the top of the nest of zoodles, sprinkle with a touch of salt.

8.    Garnish with additional black pepper and parmesan if you'd like-- we always do--and enjoy this beautiful classic dish!

| | |
|---|---|
| Calories: | 375 |
| Carbs: | 4.5g |
| Protein: | 21g |
| Fat: | 31g |

**Special Equipment:**
**Vegetable spiralizer**

Active Time: 30 minutes

Total Time: 45 minutes

# Cauliflower Gnocchi with Sage Butter

*Gnocchi is a traditional Italian potato dumpling that is made from boiled potatoes run through a ricer and mixed with flour, eggs, and salt, formed into a cylinder and then blanched in boiling water until they float. The gnocchi predates pasta and gets its name from the Italian words "nocca" meaning knuckle, mostly likely due to the shape. We adapted our gnocchi to give as much of pillowey goodness you get from potato-based gnocchi without all of those pesky carbs.*

SERVES 4

## Directions

1.  Let riced cauliflower come to room temperature and press any excess liquid out--the drier the better!
2.  Add in the egg yolks, flour, and salt, mixing thoroughly to incorporate the ingredients. Take out 1 T. of mix at a time and form them into 1/2 inch long cylinders, once you have rolled out the whole batch, gently push each one down with the back of a fork to give the gnocchi the traditional lines and to give the gnocchi a flat surface to brown on.
3.  Bring a large sauté pan to medium high heat and add 2 T. of grass-fed butter, black pepper, and the sage leaves, stir around the leaves as the butter comes to temperature. Place the gnocchi in the pan one side down (do not crowd your pan; you can do this in stages if need be) fry for 3-4 minutes until the gnocchi is brown (do not move them while you are frying them), using a spoon to carefully flip each gnocchi over and add in the other 2 T. of grass fed butter. Fry for another 4-5 minutes or until the gnocchi are golden brown and delicious.
4.  Plate the gnocchi in a large shallow bowl and garnish with the fried sage leaves from the pan, any butter left in the pan, olive oil, and parmesan cheese.

Active Time: 20 minutes

Total Time: 45 minutes

**Special Equipment:**
**Food Processor**

## Ingredients

4 C. of riced cauliflower

2 egg yolks

1tsp sea salt

1/2 tsp fresh cracked black pepper

1 C. almond flour

4 T. grass-fed butter

8 fresh sage leaves

1 T. of extra virgin olive oil (garnish)

Fresh grated parmesan cheese (garnish)

| | |
|---|---|
| Calories: | 379 |
| Carbs: | 14g |
| Protein: | 12g |
| Fat: | 34g |

# Shrimp Papardelle with Kale Pesto

*Pappardelle is a long flat noodle from the Tuscany region. Its name comes from the term "pappare" which translates into "to gobble up" and for good reason: these noodles have a ton of surface area, giving a thicker sauce the ability to stick to the outside, creating a flavor bomb in your mouth! We paired our squash Pappardelle with a walnut kale pesto to give the noodles a deep rich flavor while providing quality fats in the walnuts and olive oil.*

SERVES 4

## Preparing the Pesto

### INGREDIENTS

2 C. torn kale leaves (no stems)

1 C. basil leaves (no stems)

1/2 C. oil

1 tsp sea salt

4 cloves of garlic

Juice of one lemon

1/4 C. walnuts

### DIRECTIONS

1.    In a food processor, combine the kale leaves, basil leaves, lemon juice and salt. Pulse 10 to 12 times, until the kale leaves are finely chopped.
2.    Turn the processor back on low, slowly pouring in the olive oil to emulsify. Scrape down the sides with a rubber spatula.
3.    Add the walnuts and garlic and pulse to combine, taste and check salt for personal preference.

# GETTING IT TOGETHER

## DIRECTIONS

1.    Take a vegetable peeler and run it along the squash from top to bottom, discarding the first two pieces, continue until the squash is too small to continue. Repeat on the other squash and zucchinis; put the squash noodles in a bowl.
2.    Bring a large heavy-bottomed sauté pan to medium high heat. While the pan is heating up, take a paper towel and dab the shrimp to dry the exterior (this will help them brown nicely). Sprinkle salt and pepper on the shrimp and sear in the pan (2 minutes per side), be sure to put the shrimp in the pan and do not touch until it's time to flip. Once cooked-through (about 4 minutes) remove the shrimp from the pan and set aside.
3.    Put the zucchini noodles in the hot pan and add the water to deglaze; cover and let steam for 2 minutes. Remove the lid and add the shrimp and pesto to the pan, stir with tongs being sure to incorporate the pesto into the noodles.
4.    Use tongs to twirl the noodles into a birds nest and separate onto four plates. Arrange the shrimp around the outside of the nest and top with fresh grated parmesan cheese and cracked black pepper.

## INGREDIENTS

2 large zucchini

2 large yellow squash

1 T. fat

1/2 lb medium sized shrimp, tails off, peeled and deveined

1/4 C. of water

1 C. of Kale Pesto

Parmesan cheese to garnish

## PRO-TIP:

Make dinner easier on yourself by buying frozen, peeled and deveined shrimp and thawing them before cooking. It is still important to pat dry the outsides so they brown in the pan; drier shrimp also keep your pesto from getting too fishy.

Active Time: 20 minutes

Total Time: 30 minutes

**Special Equipment:**
**Vegetable Peeler**

| | |
|---|---|
| **Calories:** | **261** |
| **Carbs:** | **9g** |
| **Protein:** | **20g** |
| **Fat:** | **21g** |

# ZUCCHINI RAVIOLI WITH TOMATO BROTH

*We love stuffed pastas and while living a Keto, gluten-free, or paleo lifestyle means giving up the gluten, it doesn't mean you have to lose the joy of raviolis. We built these beautiful little guys to satisfy that itch, and it has become a staple at our dinner table. To offset the carbs in traditional marinara sauce, we developed this tomato infused bone broth to give the much needed flavor of a marinara sauce while adding in the highly nutrient dense broth to give you a great kick of flavor, collagen, and nutrients. This sauce works great on these raviolis and it can also be used in other applications that call for sauce like our cauliflower garlic bread or chicken Puttanesca.*

## RAVIOLI RECIPE          SERVES 4

## INGREDIENTS

2 egg yolks

1 C. whole milk full-fat ricotta cheese

½ C. grated mozzarella cheese

2 T. grated parmesan cheese

1 tsp cracked black pepper

1 tsp sea salt

1 tsp dried basil

1 tsp dried oregano

2 T. minced garlic

2 large zucchini

1 T. coconut oil

## DIRECTIONS

1.    Preheat oven to 350.
2.    Mix together in a large bowl all ingredients--except the fresh basil, coconut oil, and zucchini--and ensure the ingredients are well incorporated. Put the bowl in the fridge to keep cool while you get your zucchini ready.
3.    Put your zucchini down on your cutting board and run a vegetable peeler down the zucchini long ways to make ribbons (the first few pieces are too small to use, discard them). This requires some force, so push down hard to get the thickest ribbons your vegetable peeler will allow. Repeat this process until you have about forty solid ribbons.
4.    Place a ribbon down and another one across it to form an X, place a 1T dollop of your ricotta mixture in the center, place the top flap over the top of the ricotta dollop and then do the same with the bottom flap, it should look like a square purse, do this to all your ribbons, should yield 20 raviolis.
5.    Rub the coconut oil on a glass baking dish or non-stick cookie sheet, arrange the raviolis in the dish--it's ok to crowd the dish as long as the raviolis are not touching. Bake for 20 minutes. While the raviolis are cooking make your tomato bone broth.

| | |
|---|---|
| Calories: | 412 |
| Carbs: | 8g |
| Protein: | 21g |
| Fat: | 30g |

**Special Equipment:**
**None**

Active Time: 40 minutes

Total Time: 45 minutes

# TOMATO BONE BROTH

## DIRECTIONS

1.  Put your fat in a small sauce pan on medium high heat.
2.  Once the fat has come to temperature, add your garlic and red pepper flakes, cook for 2 minutes, or until the garlic browns just the slightest bit.
3.  Whisk in your tomato paste and cook for another 2 minutes.
4.  Deglaze with the bone broth, reduce heat to medium low, toss in your dried Italian seasoning and cook until the liquid reduces by half.

## INGREDIENTS

1tsp garlic, minced

1 tsp red pepper flakes

1 T. fat

1 T. tomato paste

2 C. bone broth (page 20,

or store bought)

1 tsp dried Italian seasoning

# PUTTING IT ALL TOGETHER

Fresh basil leaves

Fresh cracked black pepper

Extra virgin olive oil

Carefully place five raviolis on a plate--they will be delicate--and spoon generous helpings of the tomato bone broth on top. Top the ravioli with torn basil leaves, olive oil and a pinch of pepper to make a veggie-friendly showstopper!

# SECONDI

* * * * * * * * * * * * * * * * * * * * * * * * * * * * * * * * * * * * * * * * * * *

*the most substantial course of a meal.*

*If God did not intend for us to eat animals, then why did he make them out of meat?*

-John Cleese

# ROASTED COD FILLETS

*Cod is a food staple on the Italian coast, and the salt-cured variety has fed the masses of Italy for the entire history of the country. This dish utilizes the salty delicious flavor of the sea, coastal olives, and fresh citrus to let the fish shine through. This plate would be at home in any trattorie along the Italian coast—we like eating it outside on warm nights.*

SERVES 4

## INGREDIENTS

1lb of boneless cod fillets

1 tsp kosher salt

1/2 tsp freshly ground black pepper

1 T. freshly squeezed lemon juice

2 T. good olive oil

2 large sprig fresh thyme

8 large olives with pits

1 whole egg

1 tsp lemon zest

1 tsp fresh thyme leaves

## DIRECTIONS

1.    Preheat the oven to 400
2.    Place the fish fillet on a piece of parchment paper and sprinkle it with the salt and pepper. Drizzle the olive oil over the top of the fillet. Lay the thyme on top and place the olives next to the fillet.
3.    Beat the egg and brush the egg wash around the edge of the parchment paper and fold it in half. Carefully fold the edge of the parchment paper under and around the fish to make an envelope.
4.    Place the package on a sheet pan and cook for 12 to 15 minutes, until the fish is cooked through.
5.    Serve with lemon zest and thyme leaves sprinkled on top.

| | |
|---|---|
| Calories: | 170 |
| Carbs: | 1g |
| Protein: | 16g |
| Fat: | 12g |

**Special Equipment:
Parchment Paper**

Active Time: 20 minutes

Total Time: 30 minutes

# FENNEL CRUSTED CHICKEN

*A solid roasted chicken needs to be in everyone's cooking arsenal. The simplicity and deliciousness of a good yard bird can transform any dinner; this one happens to be our favorite and finds itself on our dining room table at least every other week. Be sure to buy a good quality pastured or organic chicken for the flavor and the health benefits. We like it with our Bacon Brussels Sprouts and Cauliflower Risotto.*

SERVES 4

## INGREDIENTS

1 whole chicken

**Fennel Crust**
3 T fennel seeds
3 T sea salt

## DIRECTIONS

1.   Preheat oven to 350.
2.   Toast fennel seeds for 2 minutes, then grind the fennel seeds in your spice grinder and combine with salt
3.   Rub fennel-crust mixture all over the chicken, making sure the breasts, legs and wings get nicely coated, and all the little folds in the skin are filled.
4.   Place chicken in a roasting pan on a rack and roast 60-75 minutes, breast side up, until the internal temperature is 160 degrees (be sure to check the center of the breast; avoid the bone when taking the temperature to take the proper reading after one hour).
5.   Let it rest 10-15 minutes before carving--this allows the bird to finish cooking and helps seal in the juices for a moister chicken.

## PRO-TIP:

Don't wash the chicken! The splashing water makes raw chicken germs go EVERYWHERE. Just drain any excess juices and empty the chest cavity before cooking and it's ready to go.

Active Time: 20 minutes

Total Time: 2 hours

**Special Equipment:**
**Spice Grinder**

Calories:   239
Carbs:       1g
Protein:    24g
Fat:         14g

49

# CHICKEN PUTTANESCA

*Puttanesca sauce is made of olives, anchovies, capers, tomatoes, and a little hot chili flake which helped make this dish famous the world over. All the ingredients are shelf stable and require no refrigeration. This dish is traditionally served with pasta, but Americans and Italians alike over the years have adapted this sauce to go on a lot of different items from fish and chicken, to scrambled eggs! This humble dish is thought to originate from brothels, where the ladies of the house would prepare this aromatic dish to lure in potential customers from the street. Historians have differing opinions on this origin story; regardless of where it came from it's sure to lure your family and friends into the kitchen.*

## INGREDIENTS

8 boneless chicken thighs

3 T. fat

3 cloves of garlic, minced

6 anchovy filets, diced

1 tsp red chili flake

1 T. tomato paste

1 C. bone broth

1/4 C. kalamata olives, sliced

1 T. capers

1/2 C. cherry tomatoes, quartered

8 basil leaves, torn into pieces

Salt and pepper to coat chicken

Parsley to garnish

PRO-TIP:
You can use bone in chicken thighs just add an additional fifteen minutes to the cooking time in the oven.

## DIRECTIONS

1.    Preheat the oven to 365.
2.    Place the chicken thighs down on a cutting board and season liberally with salt and pepper.
3.    Bring a heavy bottom, oven-safe sauté pan to medium high heat on the stove and add in 1 T. of fat. Once the fat has come to temperate, sear ½ of the chicken thighs on each side until brown (about 3-4 minutes per side). Set the seared chicken on a plate to the side, and repeat the process with the other half of the chicken.
4.    Once the chicken is removed from the pan, reduce heat to medium and add in the last tablespoon of fat. Add the garlic, anchovies, and red chili flakes to the pan and sauté for 2 minutes. Add in the tomato paste and bone broth, whisk to fully incorporate the tomato paste in the liquid. Add in the capers, olives, and cherry tomatoes, cook the sauce for 5 minutes, or until the liquid is reduced by half. Turn off the heat.
5.    Place the chicken thighs into the pan of sauce and spoon the sauce over the top of the chicken. Place in the oven for 25 minutes. Remove and top with the torn basil leaves and parsley, if you so desire. Put on a cooling rack or towel on the table and watch this dish disappear.

## SERVES 4

| Calories: | 419 |
|---|---|
| Carbs: | 3g |
| Protein: | 46g |
| Fat: | 22g |

**Special Equipment:**
**Oven-Safe Saute Pan**
**Or**
**Cast-iron skillet**

Active Time: 30 minutes

Total Time: 60 minutes

# FLORENTINE STEAK

*Florence is a beautiful and magical city: the architecture, the history, and the steak. The first time we saw one of these bad boys I was drooling; a gigantic three and half pound porterhouse steak on a huge wood-fired grill sizzled with its beautiful fat all over the coals...it was intoxicating. This is a fairly easy recipe to follow, but cooking the steak just right is an art form that comes with practice. The cut is something you will need to order ahead from a butcher shop or online meat store, or most local grocery stores will order/cut one for you. If you can find a dry-aged steak this is best, if not, we have directions to dry your own. This is traditionally served rare and is still wonderful all the way up to medium.*

## DIRECTIONS

1.   (If you bought a dry-aged piece you can go ahead and skip this step.) Pat the steak dry with a paper towel, wrap in cheese cloth and put on a wire rack over a sheet pan, let sit for 24 hours, change the cheese cloth and turn, let sit for another 24 hours, remove from the cheese cloth just before cooking.
2.   Get your grill hot (charcoal/wood burning is preferred, but gas or electric will work, too). Place the steak bone-down on the grill standing up in the air and let it sit for 10 minutes (you might need to babysit the steak with tongs; if your grill is slightly tilted it will fall over). This helps to relax the muscle fibers in the beef and make it extremely tender.
3.   Next lay the steak down on one side and let cook for 4 minutes (do not try to make diamonds or get fancy, you want one solid line of great grill marks), then turn and cook for three minutes on the other side of the steak. Be careful to let it brown but not burn, adjusting the cooking time as necessary.
4.   Remove from the grill and let rest for 10 minutes so you don't lose all that beautiful moisture.
5.   Sprinkle both sides of the steak with salt; slice and serve with your choice of side dishes.

### SERVES 4

## INGREDIENTS

**Steak:**
3.5 lb bone-in Porterhouse steak

1 T. coarse sea salt (to use after cooking)

**Pro-Tip Garnish: Thyme Compound Butter:**
1 stick of butter (1/2cup)
1/2 tsp salt
1 T. fresh parsley, chopped
2 tsp fresh thyme leaves
Zest of one lemon

## PRO-TIP GARNISH:

1.   Let the butter come to room temperature on the counter, add all ingredients to a stand mixer (you can use a food processor in a pinch) and thoroughly combine.
2.   Using a piece of parchment paper, wax paper, or plastic wrap, roll the butter into a log and store in the freezer until you're ready to eat!

Active Time: 30 minutes

Total Time: 1 hour/2 days

**Special Equipment:**
**Grill**
**Cheese Cloth (if needed)**

Calories:   449
Carbs:   .5g
Protein:   46g
Fat:   27g

# Osso Bucco

*Osso Bucco is another one of those super fancy sounding--and looking--dishes that is surprisingly easy to make. All the work is done early on, so set it, forget it, and reap the compliments later. Osso Bucco is traditionally made with veal, but since it's getting harder to find, more expensive to buy, and has all kinds of ethical implications, we just went with the humble pig. This may require a visit to a butcher shop or ethnic grocery store to find, as your average grocery store won't have these on their shelves--but trust us, it's totally worth making it!*

## Ingredients

4 pork shanks, 2-3" thick

Salt and fresh ground

black pepper

2 T. fat

1 yellow onion, diced

1 leek, split, cleaned and

sliced

3 ribs celery, diced

1/4 C. tomato paste

2 T. coconut flour

1 C. red wine

2 C. broth

1 bay leaf

1 tsp fresh thyme

1/2 tsp fresh rosemary

1/8 tsp ground cloves

Chopped parsley for

garnish

Fresh lemon zest for

garnish

## Directions

1.   Salt and pepper pork shanks; be sure to cover the shanks thoroughly.
2.   Heat fat in a heavy pot on high heat. Sear the pork to a nice golden brown on all sides, 3-4 minutes per side. Remove pork from pan and set aside on a plate.
3.   Reduce heat to medium and add onions, leek and celery to pot. Sprinkle 1 t. salt to help vegetables soften.
4.   Once vegetables are translucent, add tomato paste to the pot. Cook and stir until caramelized--about 4 minutes. Add coconut flour, stir for another 2 minutes, add the wine and bring to a simmer over medium-high heat.

(Recipe Continues...)

## ... DIRECTIONS

5.      Add bay leaf, thyme, rosemary, cloves, and broth to the pot and return to a simmer.

6.      Return the shanks and any juices that have accumulated back to the pot and reduce heat to a very slow simmer.

7.      Cook to fork tender--3-4 hours--depending on the size of the shank.

8.      Remove the shanks from the pot and set aside. Using an immersion blender, puree the sauce until smooth. Check the flavor for salt, pepper, and consistency; if the sauce is too thin, turn the heat up to medium high and simmer until reduced.

9.      Serve family style and enjoy the praise from your dinner guests!

## SERVES 6

## PRO-TIP:

This dish creates a cheap, easy and impressive platter for any holiday meal. We served them at Thanksgiving and received rave reviews! Use a crock-pot on low and increase the cook time for a truly tender dish.

Active Time: 30 minutes

Total Time: 4 hours

**Special Equipment:**
None

Calories:   452
Carbs:       9g
Protein:     23g
Fat:          30g

# ROASTED DUCK

*For many green chefs, the idea of roasting a whole duck can be intimidating. I'm here to tell you that it is a bit more involved than chicken, but if you want a nice bird it's not impossible by a long shot. This is a goof-proof, easy, delicious way to prepare the perfect keto poultry! Ducks, being as high in delicious fats as they are, make for the ideal ketogenic meat. Rendering out the fat as the duck is cooked also gives you a delicious base for many treats: duck fat salad dressing, duck fat fried ANYTHING and duck fat instead of butter. Let's get this roast on the road!*

SERVES 4-6

## INGREDIENTS

1 whole duck (around 4lbs)

2 T. whole coriander seeds

1/2 tsp whole black pepper

2 T. salt

1 C. water

1 lemon cut in to wedges

Juice of another lemon

1/2 C. butter

1 T. coconut flour

## DIRECTIONS

1.    Preheat oven to 325 and prepare a medium roasting pan by lining it with aluminum foil and placing a roasting rack in the pan.

2.    Remove the neck from cavity of the duck (or cut it off if it is still attached) and pat the duck dry with a paper towel.

3.    Toast half the coriander seeds in a heavy bottom pan for 2-3 minutes on medium high heat until the coriander is fragrant, remove from the heat and add the black pepper to the hot pan and let rest on the counter for 5 minutes. Grind in a mortar and pestle, spice grinder, coffee grinder or put it in a ziplock and crush the spices with something heavy.

(Recipe continues...)

(DUCK BROKEN DOWN)

## ... DIRECTIONS

4.    Season duck thoroughly with salt and coriander mixture and stuff with the lemon wedges. Pour 1 cup boiling water in the roasting pan along with remaining whole coriander seeds and duck neck.

5.    Place duck on the rack in the roasting pan and cover with aluminum foil, roast for an hour.

6.    Move duck to an aluminum foil-lined sheet pan. Pour half of the melted butter over the duck, strain and reserve drippings from the roasting pan.

7.    Turn the oven up to 350 and roast duck 45 minutes uncovered.

8.    Spoon butter and duck fat from the sheet pan over the duck again, adding extra butter as needed.

9.    Turn the oven up to 400 and roast 30-45 minutes until the skin is crispy.

10.    Remove from the oven and let the bird rest for 10 minutes before carving.

11.    Pour pan drippings back on the stove over medium heat, add in the coconut flour and stir until fully incorporated and smooth, add reserved roasting drippings and cook for 5 minutes.

12.    Add in the lemon juice, reduce to low and cook for another 5 minutes, remove from heat.

13.    Remove the lemons from the cavity of the duck; carve into eight pieces just like you would a chicken, serve on a platter with the sauce on the side.

Active Time: 30 minutes

Total Time: 2 hours 30 minutes

**Special Equipment:**
**mortar and pestle**
**OR**
**a ziplock and something to whack with**

Calories:   575
Carbs:      3g
Protein:    24g
Fat:        51g

# PORCHETTA

*Porchetta is a labor of love. It is time consuming, has lots of steps, and takes days to season, cure, and get the flavors just right. But those of us willing to put in the work will be rewarded with one of the most delicious ways to cook pork we have found in our twenty plus years of cooking. Porchetta is a celebratory dish from Rome that was used to mark holidays and feasts; we highly recommend it for your next celebration or major holiday; your guests will remember this instead of another roast turkey, we promise. Our Porchetta uses all pork belly instead of the traditional loin, belly, skin, and entrails; we wanted to preserve the dish while getting the best fat to protein ratio we could. We hope you enjoy cooking this as much as we did, testing this wonderful fat-laced beauty.*

## INGREDIENTS

3 lb piece of pork belly, skin on

2 T. fennel seeds

1 T. crushed red pepper flakes

1 T. fresh sage, minced

1 T. fresh rosemary, minced

6 garlic cloves, minced

1/2 C. kosher salt

Zest of two lemons

### SERVES 8

## DIRECTIONS

1.     Place the belly on a cutting board, push your palm down on the belly and slice a long sharp knife down the middle, bisecting it like butterflying, but all the way through. Let sit at room temperature covered in plastic for an hour. Set the top part of the belly skin side down. Using a knife, score the belly flesh in a checkerboard pattern about a ¼" deep. Flip belly, skin side up. Using a paring knife, poke dozens of 1/8"-deep holes through skin all over belly. Using a meat mallet, pound skin all over for 3 minutes to spread out and tenderize. Take the bottom part of the belly out the plastic and poke holes 1/8" deep throughout the belly, pound out for 3 minutes to spread out and tenderize.

(Recipe continued...)

| | | Special Equipment: | |
|---|---|---|---|
| Calories: | 593 | spice grinder | Active Time: 2 hours |
| Carbs: | 3g | meat mallet | |
| Protein: | 11g | butcher's twine | Total Time: 2 days |
| Fat: | 60g | | |

## ... DIRECTIONS

2.    Toast fennel seeds and red pepper flakes in a small skillet over medium heat, about 1 minute. Let cool slightly and add to a spice grinder and grind fine; mix with salt, garlic, rosemary, sage, and zest.

3.    Rub the spice blend all over the belly pieces--with the exception of skin side of the top piece. Roll the bottom portion of the belly into a roll up, as tight as you can. Now roll the top part of the belly around the bottom part you just rolled up (a roll inside a roll), now tightly tie with butcher's twine on each end and the middle. Place on a wire rack on a sheet pan and let sit uncovered in the refrigerator for 36-48 hours so the skin can properly dry.

4.    When you are ready to cook the Porchetta, let it sit outside of the refrigerator for an hour to come to room temperature, preheat the oven to 500, cook for 20 minutes and then turn rolls and cook for another 20 minutes.

5.    Reduce heat to 300 and let cook for 90 minutes, remove from the oven and let rest for 20 minutes

6.    Carve with a serrated or electric carving knife into ½" slices and serve with you choice of side dishes.

PRO-TIP:
Pat yourself on the back! If you made this, you
ARE a pro!

# CONTORNI

*a side dish of salad or vegetables that is commonly served alongside the main course.*

*Primarily I'm a meat man, although once in a while I toy with a few vegetables.*

-Nat King Cole

# ROASTED FENNEL AND ARTICHOKE

*Artichokes are an amazing vegetable for you: they help detoxify the liver and are choked full of antioxidants, making these plant hearts a super food. We use canned artichokes in this recipe because if you've ever cleaned a fresh one yourself, you will know it's not fun and barely worth the effort (in our not-so-humble opinion). Fennel is a staple in Italian cooking; it's a great source of dietary fiber, and aids in gut health. This dish combines two very healthy vegetables that you should be eating on a regular basis, and with this easy recipe you can. Now you have no excuses!*

## INGREDIENTS

2 T. coconut Oil

1 whole fennel bulb

1: 14oz can of artichokes,

quartered

1T. minced fresh garlic

1 tsp red chili flakes

1/2 tsp sea salt

1/2 tsp black pepper

2 T. Extra Virgin Olive Oil

1 T. Chopped fresh parsley

Juice of one lemon

## DIRECTIONS

1.   Preheat the oven to 400.
2.   In a pan or microwave melt the coconut oil.
3.   Remove the stalks of the fennel bulb and pull off a handful of the small leafy fronds, chop them and put 1 T. of the frond aside for garnish. Cut the bulb in half and, using the tip of a knife, cut the triangular white part of the fennel bulb out and throw it away. Chop remainder into 3/4inch wedges.
4.   Open the can of artichokes and drain well. In a bowl, mix the fennel bulb, artichokes, garlic, chili flakes, coconut oil, salt, and pepper together; add to a glass baking pan and place in the oven.
5.   Cook for 20 minutes, open the oven and stir the vegetables around a few times, bake for an additional 20 minutes.
6.   Remove from the oven and let cool for about 5 minutes. Add in the olive oil, parsley, and lemon juice; taste for salt and pepper.

| | | | |
|---|---|---|---|
| Calories: | 164 | | Active Time: 20 minutes |
| Carbs: | 9g | **Special Equipment:** | |
| Protein: | 3g | None | Total Time: 50 minutes |
| Fat: | 13g | | |

# PROSCIUTTO-WRAPPED ASPARAGUS

*This simplistic recipe is a great side dish and can also be served as an appetizer if need be. It is an elegant dish that is a go-to if you need to bring something to a party. Make sure to get your prosciutto sliced as thinly as possible; it's a balancing act to get the prosciutto crispy before you over cook the asparagus.*

## INGREDIENTS

1 bundle of medium asparagus

1/4 lb of thin sliced prosciutto

2 T. olive oil

1/2 tsp sea salt

1/2tsp fresh cracked black pepper

1 clove of garlic, crushed

## DIRECTIONS

1. Turn your oven to the low broil setting, move a rack to be about 6 inches away from the heating element.
2. Cut the last ½ inch off of the asparagus to remove the woody ends.
3. In a small bowl mix the salt, pepper, garlic, and oil together, brush on the asparagus.
4. Take the stack of prosciutto slices and cut in half horizontally, wrap the prosciutto around the center of the asparagus, place onto a sheet pan ensure you have space in between each one so they are not touching.
5. Place the sheet pan in the oven and let cook 3 minutes, pull from the oven and flip each one over, cook for an additional 3 minutes.
6. Put onto a plate and sprinkle with your favorite finishing oil, salt, or eat as is.

Active Time: 10 minutes

Total Time: 15 minutes

**Special Equipment:**
**None**

Calories:   141
Carbs:      5g
Protein:    10g
Fat:        10g

# BROCCOLI STRASCINATI

*This traditional Roman broccoli dish is one of our favorites and pairs well with almost every Secondi in this book. It's delicious and won't let you down. Feel free to substitute broccoli rabe or rapini in this dish as well, just be sure to adjust the cooking time; don't ruin your vegetables by over cooking them. That would be sad.*

## INGREDIENTS

1/4 C. coconut oil

1 lb (large bunch) broccoli

3 cloves garlic, minced

1 tsp crushed red chili flakes

1 tsp rosemary leaves

1 tsp sea salt

1 T. extra virgin olive oil

## DIRECTIONS

1.    Cut the bottom thick stem of the broccoli off, then cut the head down the center to give you two halves. Take your knife and cut the broccoli into long strips, 2-3inches long, be sure the strips are not too think--about ½ inch--to ensure proper cooking.

2.    Heat the coconut oil in a heavy bottom pan at medium-high heat, once the oil is hot add your broccoli and cook until golden brown, about 2 minutes per turn for 4 turns (total of 8 minutes).

3.    Add in all remaining ingredients except for the olive oil and stir frequently for another 2 minutes, or until the garlic has begun to brown. Remove from heat and add in the olive oil, stir, and serve.

| | | |
|---|---|---|
| **Calories:** | 167 | |
| **Carbs:** | 9g | |
| **Protein:** | 4g | |
| **Fat:** | 14g | |

**Special Equipment:**
**cast-iron skillet (optional)**

Active Time: 15 minutes

Total Time: 20 minutes

# BACON BRUSSEL SPROUTS

*Brussels sprouts...the bane of children everywhere. This wonderful vegetable has gotten a bad rap over the years due to poor cooking methods and a bad public image. These beautiful little guys provide tons of vitamin C and K along with potassium, Omega-3 fatty acids, and gut flora boosting pre-biotic fiber. This recipe with bacon and garlic provides a tasty way to include more of these healthy vegetables in your diet, while giving a bacon flavor that will please almost any dinner guest.*

## INGREDIENTS

8 slices of thick bacon cut into ¼" squares

1 lb fresh brussels sprouts

2 cloves of garlic, minced

1 T. grass-fed butter

1 tsp sea salt

1 tsp cracked black pepper

## DIRECTIONS

1. Preheat the oven to 400.
2. Put a 12" cast iron pan (or any oven safe sauté pan) on the stove on medium heat, add your bacon pieces and let cook for 8-10 minutes, stirring occasionally to render out the bacon fat.
3. While the bacon is rendering, cut off the stems of each Brussels sprout and cut in half.
4. Remove the pan from the heat and add in the garlic, salt, pepper, and the Brussels sprouts, stir until the sprouts are thoroughly coated.
5. Put the pan in the oven and cook for 10 minutes, remove from the oven and add the butter. Stir until the butter has melted and coated the sprouts, return to the oven and let cook another 5 minutes.
6. Remove from the oven and let cool for about 5 minutes before serving. Enjoy!

Active Time: 15 minutes

Total Time: 30 minutes

**Special Equipment:**
**Cast-Iron Skillet (optional)**

Calories: 132
Carbs: 7g
Protein: 8g
Fat: 9g

# FLORENTINE FIRE-GRILLED MUSHROOMS

*Mushrooms are loaded with minerals including copper, selenium, manganese and phosphorus--all the minerals your body is lacking in a ketogenic/grain-free diet. These wonder fungi can help keep you healthy and your body running properly. This is another vegetable dish that can be served on the side of any of the secondis in this book and also double as a great appetizer at a cocktail party. So the next time your annoying friend invites you to a party where "everyone brings a dish" you can make these quick delicious skewers and show them what a culinary bad ass you are.*

## INGREDIENTS

8 rosemary stalks

1 pint of crimini mushrooms

1 tsp fresh thyme leaves chopped

1 tsp balsamic vinegar

2 T. olive oil

1 tsp sea salt

1/2 tsp fresh cracked black pepper

## DIRECTIONS

1.    Place aluminum foil over part of your grill (enough to fit 8 skewers), turn your grill on to medium high heat and let it get hot.
2.    Gently remove the stems from the mushrooms and discard, clean and dry caps on the counter while you prepare the rest of the components.
3.    Remove the rosemary leaves from all but the top of the stalk leaving you with just a little on top to be decorative (save the rosemary for another dish or put in a small bottle of oil and let infuse for later).
4.    Mix the thyme leaves, balsamic, olive oil, and salt into a bowl and whisk together, toss the mushroom caps into the marinade.
5.    Skewer caps onto each rosemary skewer, making sure to leave a gap at the top and bottom as to not ruin the rosemary on top of the stalk and to leave a place to hold the skewer on the bottom.
6.    Put skewers on the aluminum foil lined grill and let cook for 4 minutes, turn and cook an additional 3 minutes, then remove from heat and serve on whatever plate you like best.

Calories:  76
Carbs:     3g
Protein:   2g
Fat:       7g

**Special Equipment:**
**grill**

Active Time: 25 minutes

Total Time: 30 minutes

# EGGPLANT ROTOLINI

*Don't skip this page! Eggplant is an often misunderstood and poorly prepared vegetable that we believe needs some more love. With the salting method in this recipe you won't find the normal bitter flavor associated with this humble vegetable, so you might find another veggie to stock in your fridge. This dish "Rotolini" is usually covered in marinara sauce, adding a lot of carbs; we decided that we would substitute the tomato topping and add everyone's favorite flavor... bacon. The dish takes on a new look and flavor profile this way and makes it special on any dinner table.*

## DIRECTIONS

1.    Cut the ends off the eggplant and slice lengthwise into 1/4 inch thick slices. You should get roughly 8 slices total. Lay slices on a rimmed baking sheet and sprinkle both sides liberally with salt--this helps to release the natural bitterness of the eggplant. Let stand for 15 minutes and then rinse salt off under cold running water and pat slices dry.
2.    Preheat the oven to 400.
3.    While the eggplant is salted and setting, pull out the bacon and cut in half horizontally to give you eight half sized pieces. Let the bacon sit out to come to room temperature.
4.    Add all other ingredients (other than the bacon) into a medium sized bowl and mix thoroughly
5.    Once the eggplant is rinsed and dry, lay them out on a cutting board and divide the stuffing into equal parts on a mound on the top of the eggplant slice, then roll up each slice into a tube. "Smoosh" the bacon with the back of a spoon to make it thinner and longer, then roll the bacon around the eggplant to cover the exterior of the roll.
6.    Place the eggplant into a glass baking dish and let cook in the oven for 20 minutes, pull out of the oven and drain any excess moisture in the pan, then put back in the oven and bake for another 10 minutes or until the bacon is crispy.
7.    Put on a platter and garnish with some grated parmesan cheese if you'd like, but they taste great on their own!

## INGREDIENTS

1 large eggplant

1 C. spinach leaves, chopped

1/2 C. of whole milk ricotta cheese

1/2 C. shredded mozzarella cheese

1 tsp garlic, minced

1 egg yolk

1 tsp dried Italian seasoning

1 tsp sea salt + 1 T sea salt

1 T. for salting the eggplant

1/2 tsp fresh cracked black pepper

4 slices of thin sliced bacon

Active Time: 30 minutes

Total Time: 1 hour

**Special Equipment:**
**none**

Calories:    181
Carbs:      9g
Protein:    11g
Fat:        12g

# CAULIFLOWER RISOTTO

*Risotto is one of the quintessential "chef" dishes; everyone has a personal touch or style to add in, making each chef's risotto a signature experience. Unfortunately, it's impossible to eat Arborio rice on a low carb diet, but that's where our trusty friend the cauliflower comes in. This is a great base recipe that makes a creamy and delicious low carb risotto that can be customized by you to make that signature dish your friends will always remember you for.*

## INGREDIENTS

1 T. coconut oil (or bacon fat)

1 medium to large head of cauliflower (4 cups of riced cauliflower)

1/2 C. diced yellow onion

2 T. minced garlic

1/2 C. chicken or vegetable broth

1/2 C. heavy cream

1/4 C. grated parmesan cheese

1 tsp thyme leaves

1 tsp salt

1 tsp fresh cracked black pepper

Finishing oil and

Parmesan cheese to garnish (opt)

## DIRECTIONS

1.    Ricing cauliflower: chop cauliflower into florets. Add the florets to your food processor and pulse until cauliflower resembles rice. How easy was that!

2.    Heat the coconut oil in a heavy-bottom pan at medium heat. Once the oil is hot, add your onion and cook until translucent, about 4 minutes. Once the onion is cooked add in the garlic and cook for an additional 2 minutes to release the flavor of the garlic.

3.    Add the cauliflower and broth to the pan, stir and cover the pan to let simmer for 10 minutes.

4.    Uncover the pan and add in the cream, thyme, salt, and pepper, raise heat to medium-high and stir frequently while the cream reduces. Once the cream is reduced by half, add in the parmesan cheese and lemon zest, stirring some more. Taste for salt; the risotto should be creamy, if it's still watery cook for a few more minutes.

5.    Spoon the risotto into a large bowl and garnish with your favorite finishing oil (we love truffle or lemon oil) and grate some fresh parmesan cheese on top.

PRO-TIP:
To customize your risotto try adding bacon, shrimp, feta cheese, blue cheese, crab, artichokes, spinach, etc... the sky is the limit, have fun creating your own signature risotto dish! For more ideas just do a quick Google search of other risotto flavors you can engineer on your own.

| | | |
|---|---|---|
| Calories: | 222 | |
| Carbs: | 9g | |
| Protein: | 5g | |
| Fat: | 20g | |

**Special Equipment:**
**none**

Active Time: 30 minutes

Total Time: 30 minutes

# UTICA GREENS

*This dish is an adaptation of Utica Greens which is an Italian-American dish made famous in New York City by Chef Joe Morelle. As we cannot use potatoes or bread crumbs on a paleo or ketogenic diet we played in the kitchen to develop a dish that had the same flavor profile and would fit into our low carb lifestyles. The bitterness of the fresh spinach, the saltiness of the prosciutto, along with the sweetness of the peppers makes this side dish a winner at every dinner we serve it.*

## INGREDIENTS

1 large bundle of fresh spinach

2 T. fat

2oz (1/4lb) prosciutto, chiffonade

4 hot cherry peppers/peppadews

1T. garlic, minced

1/2 tsp salt + 1 T. of salt

1/2 tsp fresh cracked black pepper

Parmesan cheese to garnish

## DIRECTIONS

1.   Bring a large pot of water to a boil, add in 1 T. of salt. In a separate bowl create an ice bath deep enough to fit the bundle of spinach. Blanch the spinach in the boiling water for 2 minutes (the goal is to wilt the leaves and keep some crunch in the stems), plunge the spinach into the ice bath until cool (another 2 minutes), pull the spinach out and let dry in a strainer. Give the spinach a bit of a squeeze to release more of the moisture.

2.   Bring a sauté pan to medium heat on the stove and add the fat, once the pan is at medium heat and the fat is melted, add in the garlic, prosciutto, and peppers; sauté for 5 minutes stirring often until the prosciutto is lightly browned. Add the spinach to the pan and sprinkle with the remaining salt and pepper, toss the greens around the pan for 2 minutes to incorporate the flavors and allow the spinach to get hot.

3.   Use tongs to get the spinach onto a serving platter and pour the remainder of the pan on top of the spinach and garnish with parmesan cheese.

Active Time: 15 minutes

Total Time: 20 minutes

**Special Equipment:**
none

| Calories: | 141 |
|-----------|-----|
| Carbs: | 6g |
| Protein: | 7g |
| Fat: | 11g |

# DULCE

· · · · · · · · · · · · · · · · · · · · · · · · · · · · · · · · · · · · · · · · · · · · · · · · · · · · · · · · · · · · · · · · · ·

*A sweet food or drink, especially a candy or jam.*

*We absolutely eat dessert first. The thing that you want to do most, do that!*

-Josh Whedon

# ALMOND BISCOTTI

*These are awesome little cookies to dip into coffee in the afternoons and feel like it's cheating, just a little. They also are a fancy way to finish a meal, (espresso suggested but not required) or as an accompaniment to dessert. They keep well on a plate in your coffee area for a few days and a great item to bring with you to a party if you know the host is not a low carb/gluten free kind of person.*

5/5

## INGREDIENTS

3 ¼ C. ground almond flour

1 tsp baking soda

2 tsp cinnamon

1/3 C. slivered almonds

1/4 C. flax seeds

1/4 tsp salt

2 T. Erythritol or Swerve

2 whole eggs

1 tsp vanilla extract

1 tsp almond extract

1/3 C. coconut oil

## MAKES 24 COOKIES

## DIRECTIONS

1.   Preheat oven to 325.
2.   Line a cookie sheet with parchment paper.
3.   Combine all dry ingredients in a large bowl and mix thoroughly. Meanwhile, in a separate bowl combine the eggs and extracts and whisk well, adding the egg mixture to the dry mixture and stirring to combine.
6.  In a pan--or the microwave--heat the coconut oil until warm (not hot) and liquefied. Add the oil to the mix and incorporate until well mixed.
7.  Pour the batter onto the cookie sheet and form a loaf 3/4" thick and 4" wide.
8.  Place in the oven and bake for 25 minutes, until golden brown.
8.  Remove from the oven and wait for them to cool down to room temperature, then lower the oven temperature to 300.
10. Slice the loaf into 1/2-3/4" long sticks, place cookies back into the oven for 20-30 minutes, until your personal optimum crunchiness level is achieved, remove and let cool.

| Calories: | 130 |
|---|---|
| Carbs: | 4g |
| Protein: | 4g |
| Fat: | 12g |

**Special Equipment:**
**Parchment Paper**

Active Time: 30 minutes

Total Time: 2 hours

PRO-TIP 1:
Once biscotti are cooled, melt 1/4 C. DARK
sugar free chocolate chips (80% cocoa) with 1 T.
coconut oil in the microwave until melted. Dip,
drizzle or spoon chocolate over half of each
biscotti and cool until chocolate sets. You can
also sprinkle some pistachios or macadamia nuts
on the chocolate to make this a decadent dessert.

PRO-TIP 2:
Sprinkle flaked sea salt on the chocolate while
it's setting for a more upscale looking biscotti.

# KETOMISU

*Tiramisu is the quintessential Italian dessert. It's a creamy, spiked, espresso-laced, and cocoa-topped dreamboat of a dessert that is always a crowd pleaser. We spent weeks trying to make a great low carb lady finger, but none of the recipes we tried really gave us what we were looking for. So, after many nights of delicious and indulgent experimentation we decided to use our almond biscotti recipe instead of the lady fingers. This allowed us to keep the carbs low and the flavor and texture on point! If you do not own an espresso maker no worries, stop at any coffee shop (some have even have a drive through!) and get a double espresso, bring it home and let it sit on the counter until you are ready to use it.*

## INGREDIENTS

**Custard:**

6 egg yolks

3 T. Erythritol or Swerve

8 ounces mascarpone cheese

2 C. heavy cream

**Assembly:**

10 Almond Biscottis (Page 70)

Custard recipe from above

2 shots of chilled espresso

2 T. dark rum

1 tsp dark cocoa powder

**SERVES 10**

## DIRECTIONS

1.   In small mixing bowl, beat egg yolks, erythritol and stevia until thick and lemon colored.
2.   Place mixture on top of a double boiler over boiling water. Reduce heat to low. Cook 8-10 minutes, stirring constantly. Remove from heat. Add mascarpone cheese, beating well.
3.   In a small mixing bowl, beat heavy or whipping cream in a stand mixer until stiff peaks form. Fold into egg yolk mixture; place in refrigerator until you are ready to assemble.

1.   Mix the rum and espresso together in a bowl, take a pastry brush and brush the mixture over the biscotti on both sides to coat.
2.   Place half the biscotti on the bottom of a 8x4 glass loaf pan or other similarly sized pan, cover with half of the custard mix, place the second half the biscotti on top of that and top with the remaining custard mix
3.   Sprinkle the cocoa powder on top of custard and set in the refrigerator until ready to serve.

PRO-TIP:
To make the presentation even sexier you can crumble up the biscotti in a ziploc bag and build the Keto-Misu in a martini glass. Cover the bottom with some chilled espresso, next add some biscotti crumbs, then some custard, and then top with more biscotti crumbs and the cocoa powder. Great for a Keto date night!

| | |
|---|---|
| Calories: | 448 |
| Carbs: | 6g |
| Protein: | 4g |
| Fat: | 32g |

**Special Equipment:**
**Glass Loaf Pan**
**Stand Mixer/Hand Mixer**

Active Time: 40 minutes

Total Time: 1 hour

# AFFOGATO WITH FAT-BOMB ICE-CREAM

*Wait, did the title say "ice-cream"? On a Ketogenic diet?!? Yes, the below recipe is for fat bomb ice-cream that actually contains no cream at all. It sounds strange when you read the ingredients, but trust me this recipe is amazing and the results are great, just be aware of how much fat is in this recipe and don't eat it all in one sitting. Affogato translates to "drowned", which makes sense as with this delicious dessert you are going to drown this amazing fat bomb ice-cream with dark Italian espresso (or strong coffee). Folks argue over whether this is a beverage or dessert and where on a menu to put it; we say, who gives a sh\*t and enjoy!*

## DIRECTIONS

1.     Add all ingredients--except the lime juice & water--to a blender and blend until the mixture is smooth (it will take some time for the butter to break down and get creamy). After about a minute add in the lime juice & water slowly to help emulsify the mixture and loosen it up. Taste a little with your finger to check the sweetness level, add more sweetener if you'd prefer.
2.     Pour the mixture into your ice cream maker and follow the manufacturer's instructions.
3.     Put in the freezer to store. Pull out and let soften for twenty minutes on the counter before serving

ASSEMBLY:
1.     Put a 2oz scoop of fat bomb ice-cream in the bottom of a wide mouthed coffee mug, pour a shot of espresso or 3oz of strong dark coffee over the ice-cream.
2.     Garnish with the macadamia nut mixture if you'd like, but the fat bomb ice-cream and espresso are delicious on their own.

## INGREDIENTS

4 whole eggs

4 egg yolks

2 tsp good quality vanilla extract

Juice ½ of a lime

7 T. grass-fed butter

7 T. coconut oil

3 T. MCT oil

4 T. of Xylitol or Swerve sweeteners

1/4 tsp sea salt

½ C. cold water

PRO-TIP GARNISH:

**1/4 C. macadamia nuts
4 dark chocolate covered espresso beans**

Put the espresso beans and macadamia nuts in a spice grinder, dry blender, or coffee grinder and pulse about ten times.

Active Time: 20 minutes

Total Time: 45 minutes

**Special Equipment:
Ice-cream maker and blender**

| | |
|---|---|
| **Calories:** | **243** |
| **Carbs:** | **2g** |
| **Protein:** | **3g** |
| **Fat:** | **25g** |

# CANNOLI BITES

*I loved going to the local bakery as kid and getting a Cannoli. Not having a big sweet tooth, I loved that these burrito looking pastries were not too sweet and had a variety of toppings; some had chocolate, some pistachios, others with almonds. We adapted the cannoli into a bite sized cup for this recipe; it's low carb, delicious, and can be made ahead of time to bring to a party or to keep around for a holiday gathering.*

## INGREDIENTS

2 C. almond flour

4 T. Erythritol or Swerve

1/2 tsp cinnamon

1/2 tsp dark cocoa powder

1/4 C. melted butter

1 egg

1/8 tsp salt

1 T. marsala wine

# MAKING THE CRUST

## DIRECTIONS

1.    Preheat oven to 350. In a large mixing bowl, add all ingredients above and mix until well incorporated.

2.    Spray mini muffin pan with nonstick cooking spray. Press cup mixture into mini tin making a large depression in the middle to fit the cannoli cream, (I found the back of a 1/2T measuring spoon worked great).

3.    Bake for 15 minutes and then let cool.

# FILLING IT UP

## DIRECTIONS

1.    Put all ingredients into a mixing bowl and whip with a hand mixer or stand mixer for 2 minutes. You want it nice and fluffy!
2.    Place in the fridge until the cups have come to room temperature, pipe the cream into the cups and top with your choice of: dark chocolate chips (no sugar added of course), chopped pistachios, macadamia nuts, unsweetened coconut flakes, or slivered almonds.

## INGREDIENTS

2 C. of ricotta cheese

1/2 C. sweetener

1 tsp vanilla extract

1 tsp almond extract

Zest of 1 lemon

## PRO-TIP:

Put the cream mixture in a Ziploc bag, let cool in the fridge and then cut the bottom tip off one side of the bag and use it as a piping bag. No bag or tip necessary, but it does look cooler if you use one.

## MAKES 24 BITES

Active Time: 30 minutes

Total Time: 1 hour

**Special Equipment:**
mixer
**mini muffin Pan**

Calories:   111
Carbs:        3g
Protein:      5g
Fat:            9g

# LEMON BASIL PANNA COTTA

*This is a really elegant and delicious dessert that is almost as easy to make as Jello! Panna Cotta is rich, creamy, and full of fat; almost like a custard. We like pairing it with bright refreshing flavors and colors to offset the richness. Panna Cotta can even be frozen to enjoy later, as long as you don't skip the refrigeration stage.*

## PANNA COTTA

### INGREDIENTS

1 package unflavored gelatin

2 T. cold water

2 C. heavy cream

1 C. half & half

10 basil leaves

3 T. Erythritol or Swerve

1 tsp vanilla extract

Zest of one lemon

### DIRECTIONS

1.	Sprinkle gelatin in a small saucepan over cold water, raise the heat until gelatin is dissolved completely and remove from heat (do not simmer or boil, you will ruin your gelatin).
2.	In a medium saucepan bring cream, half & half, Erythritol, vanilla extract and basil leaves just to a boil, stirring. Throw basil stems in as well--if you feel extra lazy, just toss the sprig in whole. Turn off heat and let basil steep 5-10 minutes, strain out the basil leaves and stems and add in the gelatin mixture from step one and the fresh lemon zest.
3.	Divide into ramekins, mason jars, rocks glasses or in extreme desperation, shot glasses, with 1/4" of room left at the top.
4.	Chill at least 3 hours in your refrigerator.

### YIELDS 8 SERVINGS

Calories:	258
Carbs:	6g
Protein:	2g
Fat:	27g

**Special Equipment:**
none
blender (for gelee)

Active Time: 30 minutes

Total Time: 6 hours

# Pro-Tip Gelee

## Directions

1.   Sprinkle gelatin in a small saucepan over cold water, raise the heat until gelatin is dissolved completely and remove from heat (do not simmer or boil, you will ruin your gelatin).
2.   Place the berries and lemon juice into a blender and blend until liquefied, strain into the gelatin mixture from step one.
3.   Spoon a small amount of gelee on top of the already chilled panna cotta and chill for another two hours or overnight.
4.   Serve with a sprig of fresh mint or on its own!

## Ingredients

10-12 blackberries

1 C. fresh lemon juice

1 package gelatin

2 T. cold water

# Menus

●●●●●●●●●●●●●●●●●●●●●●●●●●●●●●●●●●●●●●●●●●●●●●●●●●●●●●●●●

*A multi-coursed meal is a labor of love that you get to share with the people you hold most dear--or, a spiteful task of glee that you can perform on that annoying friend who always seems to make the best food at their parties (how do you like that, Stacey!) A large meal that lasts for hours is a lost art in the American landscape, but a tradition in Italy. In our not-so-humble opinion we think this a great way to spend a Saturday or Sunday, especially with some dry red wine or cocktails. We separated out meal plans into three levels so you can work your way up each time to a more complicated and impressive meal.*

| Beginner | Intermediate | Advanced |
|---|---|---|
| **Starter** *Antipasto board* | *Antipasto* *Chicken Liver Pate with Keto Crostini* | *Antipasto:* *Keto Garlic Bread with Tomato Bone Broth* |
| **Salad** *Caprese* | *Zuppa* *Mushroom Cheese Fonduta* | *Insalata* *Keto Kale Caesar with Chia Seed Croutons* |
| *Pasta Course* *Shrimp Pappardelle with Kale Pesto* | *Primi* *Keto Carbonara* | *Primi* *Cauliflower Gnocchi with Sage Brown Butter* |
| *Main Course* *Fennel Crusted Chicken with* | *Secondi and Contorni* *Florentine Steak Cauliflower Risotto Prosciutto Asparagus* | |
| *Florentine Fire Grilled Mushrooms and Bacon Brussels sprouts* | *Dolce* *Cannoli Bites* | *Secondi and Contorni* *Osso Bucco Broccoli Strascinati Eggplant Rotolini* |
| *Dolce* *Lemon Basil Panna Cotta* | | *Dolce* *Keto-Misu* |

# Expert Menu for Holidays and Large Gatherings

........................................................

*This is our holiday meal menu for your next large family gathering or holiday at your house. The menu might look overwhelming at first, but the dishes are arranged to help you maximize your oven space, time, and impact to make this a one of a kind holiday meal that no one will forget.*

# Antipasti
Antipasto Board with Grilled Vegetables
Chicken Liver Pate with Keto Crostini
Asparagus wrapped in Prosciutto
Florentine Mushroom Skewers

# Main Course *Serve Family Style for 8-10 people*
Keto Kale Caesar with Chia Seed Croutons
Caprese
Vegetable Lasagna
Porchetta
Whole Roasted Cod Fillets
Roasted Artichokes and Fennel
Eggplant Rotolini
Bacon Brussels Sprouts

# Dolce
Keto-Misu
Cannoli Bites
Almond Biscotti
Coffee

# PREP TWO DAYS AHEAD OF TIME

*To attack this meal you will need to start two days ahead of time (just like your mom or grandma did/do before the holidays). This will give you a ton of time on the day of your gathering, as well as make your life a lot easier (it's so much easier to cook when you house is quiet and empty).*

## **Two Days ahead of time**
*Porchetta \*preparation\**

*Almond Biscotti X2 (one recipe for the Keto-Misu, one to serve on its own)*

# **DAY AHEAD PREP**

*Chicken Liver Pate*
*Keto-Crostini*
*Keto-Caesar Dressing*
*Chia Seed Croutons*
*Vegetable Lasagna (save the final cooking step until tomorrow)*
*Keto-Misu*
*Cannoli Bites*

***Be sure to store your pate, dressing, lasagna, cannoli bites, and keto-misu covered in the refrigerator overnight; store the croutons and crostini in ziploc bags on the counter.***

# DAY OF COOKING

## *Antipasti*

Grill Vegetables (While prepping this also prep your eggplant for the rotolini)
Anti-Pasti Board
Asparagus wrapped in Prosciutto
Florentine Mushroom Skewers

We recommend you put the anti-pasti course out when guests start to arrive, this will give them something to nibble on while you finish cooking.

## *Main Course \*Serve Family Style\**

Assemble Keto Kale Caesar with Chia Seed Croutons
Caprese
Final Cooking step for the Vegetable Lasagna
Cook the Porchetta
Whole Roasted Cod Fillets
Roasted Artichokes and Fennel
Eggplant Rotolini
Bacon Brussels Sprouts

Serve the meal family style, on the table and let everyone help themselves, this makes life much easier for you and everyone gets to be involved!

## *Dolce*

Set out the Biscotti and Cannoli bites on trays
Slice and serve the Keto-Misu
Coffee

# Thanks for Reading!

● ● ● ● ● ● ● ● ● ● ● ● ● ● ● ● ● ● ● ● ● ● ● ● ● ● ● ● ● ● ● ● ● ● ● ● ● ● ● ● ● ● ● ● ● ● ● ● ●

*If you are looking for more recipes, tips, biohacks, or just want to see what we are up to, head on over to:*

*www.counterpointnutrition.com*

*Thanks to all our wonderful readers, friends, and family who not only make out lives possible, but make our food better with the seasonings of smiles, love, and laughter.*

77358257R00049

Made in the USA
Lexington, KY
26 December 2017